WACKY WAVING

inflatable

TUBE GAL

A HERSTORY

T0364084

RP Minis®
Hachette Book Group
1290 Avenue of the Americas, New York, NY 10104
www.runningpress.com
@Running_Press

First Edition: September 2021

Published by RP Minis, an imprint of Perseus Books, LLC, a subsidiary of Hachette Book Group, Inc. The RP Minis name and logo is a trademark of the Hachette Book Group.

The publisher is not responsible for websites (or their content) that are not owned by the publisher.

ISBN: 978-0-7624-7346-5

CONTENTS

INTRODUCTION

Ah, Wacky Waving Inflatable Tube Guys. You've seen them everywhere, gyrating wildly and beckoning you into cell phone stores, job fairs, mattress warehouses, and more. These wacky dudes bring joy everywhere they wave and are beloved the world over, and for good reason—they are basically happiness incarnate.

However, a recent discovery has shocked keen fans of these endlessly undulating chutes. Scientists studying the world-famous Wacky Waving Inflatable Tube Guy have compiled new evidence that proves it's not just an army of Tube *Guys* thrashing around in front of strip malls, but also Tube *Gals*! They were blown away.

This new discovery has opened our eyes to a whole new perspective on tube people.

We are excited to introduce here for the first time ever:

TULIP, THE WACKY WAVING INFLATABLE TUBE GAL!

Move over, tube dudes—there's a new tube in town.

TULIP THE TUBE GAL
• ORIGIN STORY •

Brilliant Trinidadian artist Peter Minshall first designed gigantic 60-foot-tall tube people—each with two legs, two arms, and heads full of streamers—to wow the crowd at the 1998 NFL Super Bowl XXXII half-time show. Scientific understanding of the tube people began to evolve upon closer examination of footage from this event. Scientists narrowed

their focus on the purple tube person in videos from the halftime show, as the tube's unique dancing style and funky moves caught their eye. Once they realized what they had discovered, they pored over footage from other events in which Tube Guy performed (see pages 12–14 for a recap of this history) and saw the same unique motion. It appears that Tube Gals have existed for as long as Wacky Waving Inflatable Tube People have been around.

Tube enthusiasts (en-tube-thiasts?) are committed to continuing their research to discover even more types of tube people. We may not know everything about this unique group, but one thing is clear: within the rainbow of colors present in these people, there is surely a beautiful and diverse range of characters.

TUBE PEOPLE THROUGH THE AGES

. . . .

You wouldn't believe all the crazy things tube people have gotten up to!

1996 Atlanta Olympics Opening Ceremony: In their first public appearance, dozens of 60-foot-tall, tube-shaped figures provide a spectacular backdrop for opening night of athletics' biggest competition. Gold medal!

1998 NFL Super Bowl XXXII half-time show: Football got in on the action as a bunch of multicolored dancing tube people joined mega-watt stars for a Motown-themed performance. Touchdown!

1998 Grammy Awards Performance: Tube people graced the Grammy stage with arguably the most popular Latino singer of the 1990s—Ricky Martin. *Bailamos!*

1998 to present: The larger-than-life creations begin to shrink in stature and take over the world's advertising landscape. Sellouts!

2018: The world's first miniature, desktop *Wacky Waving Inflatable Tube Guy* hits shelves. Tubular!

2021: Tulip becomes the first female tube person to receive the honor of being miniaturized. Trailblazer!

THE TUBE PEOPLE ETHOS

There is so much more to tube people than just being wacky and dancing so *craAaAzY*! They have lives and families of their own and choose a variety of professions, from surgeons to Steadicam operators. But a huge number of these characters go into the marketing, back-up dancing, and general "hype person" industries because they are a selfless, passionate, and hardworking people. They are attracted to roles where they can draw your attention to the wonders of the world, no matter how small or insignificant they might seem. Just as in a gathering of a rainbow assortment of tube people, there is beauty everywhere—and they're here to help showcase it.

In recent years, the tube people have danced their way into pop-culture legend and seriously impressive job placements. As you pass yet another tube person on the side of the road beckoning you into a Christmas decoration close-out sale, you might wonder, *Who's doing marketing for the tube people?* But that's the thing—when they're out there "getting jiggy with it," they're marketing not only for their employers, but also for their people as a whole. This, researchers now believe, is the reason behind their ubiquity: they are committed to going above and beyond for their clients, but they aren't afraid to pump up their own reputation, too.

Like humans, tube people all experience personal and professional setbacks from time to time. However, they try to stay flexible when faced with adversity; when a storm rolls in, they might bend with the wind, but they never break. Tube people try to just keep on keepin' on, no matter what life throws at them.

As such, through their decades of experience, the tube people have developed an ethos that we can all aspire to: **Be flexible. Don't let problems deflate you. Stay pumped, and always keep dancing!**

We could all learn a thing or two from Tube Gals, Guys, and their brethren!

YOUR VERY OWN
TUBE GAL
• USES •

You may already have a mini Wacky
Waving Inflatable Tube Guy (hey,
Toby!), and maybe you've put him to
use as a tiny marketing tool for your
latest achievement, a scarecrow for
your office plants, a wee dance
instructor, or a white noise machine
for your office naps. Feel free to use
Tulip for any of those tasks, too, but

here are a few fun ways to utilize her
unique set of skills or to use a whole
gaggle of tube people together:

Portable cheering section: Give yourself some much-needed encouragement at the office when you finally tackle your to-do list or at home when you vacuum for the first time in three months. Ew!

Mini disco dance party: Gather Tulip, Toby, and all their buds for the hottest dance party in town! See? You have friends!

Your biggest (well, actually smallest) fan: Obviously Tulip supports you, but she can also literally double as a personal cooling device when you overheat after walking up the stairs. Fitness!

Video conference back-up dancers: Liven up your two-hour virtual meeting that could have been an email. Synergy!

Cat entertainment: Place Tulip on the other side of a window to keep your cats (I can't believe you have eleven cats) entertained for hours! Me-ow!

Giant Tube Gal for bugs: Treat the inhabitants of your ant farm to the glorious wonder of a giant Tube Gal. Perspective!

SETTING UP

. . . .

Time to get this desktop party started!

Refer to the enclosed Power Supply information sheet and choose your form of power (9-volt battery or AC/DC adapter).

Pick an appropriate dance floor for your gal to do her thing (your boss's desk, perhaps?). Almost ready!

Turn the base fan switch to "DC" or "BATTERY" depending on your power supply. She is literally a dancing machine!

This book has been bound using handcraft methods and Smyth-sewn to ensure durability.

Illustrated by Gemma Correll.

Designed by Jenna McBride.

Written by Conor Riordan.